Jacob's Day

Lily Richardson

These are all the things Jacob did today.
At what time did he do these things?

ride a bike

eat lunch

water the garden

eat dinner

eat breakfast

play basketball

3

Jacob ate his breakfast at **8:00**.

Jacob rode his bike at **10:00**.

Jacob ate his lunch at **12:00**.

Jacob watered the garden at **2:00**.

Jacob played basketball at **4:00**.

Jacob ate his dinner at **6:00**.

Jacob's Day

8:00

10:00

12:00

2:00

4:00

6:00